Come to the Cross

Daily Devotionals for Easter

Kelly Wenner

Come to the Cross Easter Devotionals
Written by Kelly Wenner
Copyright © 2025 by SoulStrength Fit
All rights reserved.

For permission requests, contact:

SoulStrength Fit
www.soulstrengthfit.com
ISBN: 979-8-9929143-0-6

Contents

Welcome to Come to the Cross

Daily Devotionals for Easter

We are invited to come to the cross and listen to Jesus' last words during His final hours. Lean in closely and hear the message Jesus has for you in each of His final statements. Next week, we'll step back and journey through the final days leading up to our Lord's triumph and resurrection.

The Seven Last Statements of Jesus

- **"Father, forgive them, for they do not know what they are doing."** – Luke 23:34
- **"My God, my God, why have you forsaken me?"** – Matthew 27:46; Mark 15:34
- **"Truly I tell you, today you will be with me in paradise."** – Luke 23:43
- **"Father, into your hands I commit my spirit."** – Luke 23:46
- **"Woman, here is your son"** … **"Here is your mother."** – John 19:26-27
- **"I am thirsty."** – John 19:28
- **"It is finished."** – John 19:30

For a deeper experience that strengthens both body and spirit, consider pairing these devotionals with the *Come to the Cross* faith-based fitness workout program from SoulStrength Fit.

This program includes faith-centered workouts that align with the devotionals, encouraging growth in both physical health and spiritual focus. Visit www.soulstrengthfit.com to learn more.

Let's begin this journey together—pursuing a deeper connection with God as we come to the cross and hear what Jesus is saying to each of us personally.

Week 1
Devotionals

Day 1: Father, Forgive Them

"Father, forgive them, for they do not know what they are doing." – Luke 23:34

Read: Luke 23:1-34

Just days before, crowds had lined the streets of Jerusalem, joyfully welcoming Jesus as He entered the city mounted on a donkey.

"The next day the large crowd that had come to the feast heard that Jesus was coming to Jerusalem. So they took branches of palm trees and went out to meet him, crying out, 'Hosanna! Blessed is he who comes in the name of the Lord, even the King of Israel!' And Jesus found a young donkey and sat on it, just as it is written: 'Fear not, daughter of Zion; behold, your king is coming, sitting on a donkey's colt!'"
– John 12:12-15 (ESV)

Every devout Jew would have recognized the significance of Jesus' entrance—fulfilling the prophecy of the coming King.

Read: Zechariah 9:9

But the celebration was short-lived. By Thursday evening, Jesus was betrayed by a friend, arrested, mocked, beaten, abandoned, and denied—even by His most loyal disciple, Peter.
He was flogged, ridiculed, stripped of His clothes, and led to the place of His execution.
It is here that we meet Jesus now. It is here that we come to the cross and listen to His final words.

5

"Father, forgive them, for they do not know what they are doing."
We begin with Jesus' staggering statement of radical forgiveness. In the very act of His brutal execution, He prays for those harming Him. In these words, we see the depth of God's love for humanity and the embodiment of everything Jesus taught about forgiveness.

Read: Luke 6:27-36

Even after betrayal, beatings, mockery, and unimaginable suffering, Jesus prays for forgiveness—for those who have wronged Him.

But who is *they*?
"They" includes the soldiers who nailed Him to the cross.
"They" includes the crowd that turned from praising Him to shouting for His death.
"They" includes Herod, who mocked Him.
"They" includes Pilate, who gave in to public pressure.
"They" includes the religious leaders who plotted against Him.
But could *they* include us as well?
When Jesus prays, **"Father, forgive them, for they do not know what they are doing,"** is He also praying for you and me?
Have you ever considered yourself among those who helped crucify Jesus? Why or why not?

One of Jesus' disciples betrayed Him. Ten deserted Him. One denied knowing Him. Only one remained to witness His crucifixion. In what ways have you ever deserted or denied Jesus in your life?

We crucify Jesus when our words and actions fail to align
with our faith.
We crucify Jesus when we rationalize sin or ignore how our
actions affect others.
We must recognize the ways we, too, have fallen short—and
receive the forgiveness Jesus freely offers. Through His
sacrifice, God invites us into a life of love, mercy, and grace.

*"For if, while we were God's enemies, we were reconciled to him through
the death of his Son, how much more, having been reconciled, shall we be
saved through his life!"*
– Romans 5:10

*"He canceled the record of the charges against us and took it away by
nailing it to the cross."*
– Colossians 2:14

Before we received the forgiveness found at the cross, we
were enemies of God. It's easy to minimize or resist this
truth—but when we do, we also diminish the depth of what
Jesus has done for us.
Yet, because of His sacrifice, we are now **fully
forgiven** and **reconciled** to God.

With this idea of reconciliation in your mind, read this
passage from Colossians (MSG):

*"All the broken and dislocated pieces of the universe—people and
things, animals and atoms—get properly fixed and fit together in vibrant
harmonies, all because of his death, his blood that poured down from the
cross.
You yourselves are a case study of what he does. At one time you all had
your backs turned to God, thinking rebellious thoughts of him, giving
him trouble every chance you got. But now, by giving himself completely
at the Cross, actually dying for you, Christ brought you over to God's
side and put your lives together, whole and holy in his presence.*

You don't walk away from a gift like that! You stay grounded and steady in that bond of trust, constantly tuned in to the Message, careful not to be distracted or diverted."

You are forgiven. You are reconciled with God. You are whole and holy in His presence.
How easily do you accept this truth—that you are whole and holy in God's sight?

Is it harder for you to believe that you were once an enemy of God, or that you are now fully reconciled? Why?

You are not defined by your worst mistakes. Because of Jesus, you stand before God holy and pure. You are growing into the image of Christ every day.
Transformation takes time. Often, we don't notice the changes happening in us.

Reflecting on your faith journey, what is one gradual but significant change you have experienced?

How can this encourage you in the areas of your life where change still feels slow?

Take a moment to sit with the Lord. Where is He encouraging you today? Where is He calling you to trust in His grace and walk in the fullness of His forgiveness?

Close your time in prayer, thanking Jesus for His mercy and asking Him to shape you into His image more each day. Surrender your heart to Him, and rest in the truth that you are fully forgiven, fully loved, and fully His.

Day 2: My God, Why Have You Forsaken Me

"My God, my God, why have you forsaken me?"
– Mark 15:34

Read: Mark 15:1-41

In the midst of His pain and agony, Jesus turns to prayer. This was His regular practice, as we see throughout Scripture. He withdrew from the crowds to pray, spent time alone with the Father often, and prayed with His disciples frequently. His last act before His arrest was leading His disciples to the Mount of Olives so He could pray. It is no surprise, then, that His final words included prayer.

"Eloi, Eloi, lema sabachthani?" (which means *"My God, my God, why have you forsaken me?"*)

What a deep, heartfelt cry—Jesus expressing His feeling of being forsaken by God.
Have you ever felt forsaken by God? Have you ever felt forgotten, abandoned, or unheard? Is there a time when you felt God was far away?

But why would Jesus, who is God—who is part of the Holy Trinity—feel abandoned by God?

Susan Robb writes in *Seven Words*:
"While I think these words are difficult for us to hear, they are also some of the most endearing words of Jesus because they most clearly reveal his

9

humanity. In this moment, he is just like us—not simply in that he shared our human physical needs for food, water, sleep, and shelter. In this moment, he is also like us in that he feels what we have all felt: humiliation, betrayal, pain, suffering, abandonment—godforsakenness."

In His darkest moment, Jesus doesn't turn away from God. He doesn't deny His existence. Instead, He turns to Him with an honest prayer: *Where are You? Why haven't You come to help Me?*
Jesus knew His story wouldn't end at the cross. He had already told His disciples and prepared them for what was to come—that He would be handed over to the authorities, crucified, and raised on the third day.

But by quoting these words from Psalm 22**,** He shows us that He understands our pain and suffering. He understands what it feels like to question, to feel abandoned. When we walk through dark valleys—through pain, despair, and isolation—Jesus' words remind us: "I have been there. I understand."

"Eloi, Eloi, lema sabachthani?" (*"My God, my God, why have you forsaken me?"*)
Spoken in His native Aramaic, Jesus cries out in prayer with the opening words of Psalm 22**.**

Read: Psalm 22

(Take note of the similarities to the crucifixion narrative.)
The psalm begins with David's agonized cry, expressing his own experience of feeling abandoned by God. He describes his worst suffering—not only that enemies surround him and his body is wracked with pain, but that he feels as if God does not hear him, as if He has turned away.
This was David's experience.
This was Jesus' experience.

And this is the experience of many of God's people in times of deep distress, pain, or despair.

We wonder why God is not coming to our aid when we are suffering. We feel abandoned.

But when we examine Psalm 22 beyond the opening verse that Jesus quotes, we gain insight into His heart in that moment.

If Jesus had spoken the entire psalm, we would have also heard these words:

"In You our ancestors put their trust;
they trusted, and You delivered them." – Psalm 22:4

Jesus knew God hears His people. He knew He was not forgotten.

And later in the psalm, we read:
"Those who suffer will eat and have enough. Those who look for the Lord will praise Him. May your heart live forever! All the ends of the earth will remember and turn to the Lord. All the families of the nations will worship before Him. For the holy nation is the Lord's, and He rules over the nations.
All the proud ones of the earth will eat and worship.
All who go down to the dust will fall to their knees before Him—even he who cannot keep his soul alive.
Future generations will serve Him; they will tell of the Lord to their children.
They will come and proclaim His righteousness to a people yet to be born—for He has done it."
– Psalm 22:26-31 (NLV)

This was the psalm that carried Jesus through to His final moments. Jesus' cry was not just a lament of abandonment—it was a declaration of victory.
This psalm, which He quoted from the cross, was not about being forsaken forever.
It was a **song of triumph**. How do His words speak to you?

Day 3: You Will Be With Me in Paradise

"Truly I tell you, today you will be with me in paradise." – Luke 23:43

Read: Luke 23:32-43

"One of the criminals who hung there hurled insults at him: 'Aren't you the Messiah? Save yourself and us!'"

The word *Messiah* was familiar to every Jewish person. It referred to the one chosen by God to save His people. But in this moment, the criminal on the cross turns the title into an insult.
How could the Savior of the world be hanging on a cross, helpless and dying?

He wasn't the only one to mock Jesus. The religious leaders, the soldiers, and the crowd all sneered at Him as He hung beneath the sign that read: "This is the King of the Jews."
But the other criminal had a different response.

"But the other criminal rebuked him. 'Don't you fear God,' he said, 'since you are under the same sentence? We are punished justly, for we are getting what our deeds deserve. But this man has done nothing wrong.' Then he said, 'Jesus, remember me when you come into your kingdom.'"

Compare this response with Matthew's account:

"Two rebels were crucified with him, one on his right and one on his left. Those who passed by hurled insults at him, shaking their heads and saying, 'You who are going to destroy the temple and build it in three days, save yourself! Come down from the cross, if you are the Son of God!'
In the same way the chief priests, the teachers of the law, and the elders mocked him. 'He saved others,' they said, 'but he can't save himself! He's the king of Israel! Let him come down now from the cross, and we will believe in him. He trusts in God. Let God rescue him now if He wants him, for he said, 'I am the Son of God.'
In the same way, the rebels who were crucified with him also heaped insults on him." – Matthew 27:38-44

Something must have changed in the mind of the second criminal.
At first, he joined in the insults. But now, hanging next to Jesus in his final moments, he has a new understanding.
Instead of mocking, he asks Jesus to remember him when He enters His kingdom.
Picture this criminal in your mind—hanging from the cross, facing death, and yet in that moment, becoming a believer.
What do you think he was guilty of? What crime could he have committed to be sentenced to crucifixion?

"We are punished justly, for we are getting what our deeds deserve."

Do you think the criminal was speaking about punishment from Rome—or from God?

This man, suffering the same brutal execution as Jesus, overheard Him pray:
"Father, forgive them, for they do not know what they are doing."

Perhaps he had seen Jesus teach before, or witnessed His miracles. Perhaps, in this moment, Jesus' words finally made sense.

While others mocked, he saw Jesus' innocence. He recognized Jesus as King, believing that His crucifixion would not end His kingdom, nor prevent it from coming.

"Jesus, remember me when you come into your kingdom."

These are not just words pleading for his suffering to end. What makes this a statement of faith?

We see from these two criminals two very different responses to suffering:

- We can turn against God, saying: *"If You are so great, powerful, and loving, why aren't You helping me?"*

- Or, we can turn to God, acknowledging our sin and crying out for mercy.

Perhaps Luke includes this moment to teach us that there is great reward in responding to suffering as the second criminal did.

"Jesus, remember me when you come into your kingdom."

Susan Robb writes in *Seven Words*:

"Asking to be remembered by God is, in itself, a request for deliverance or salvation—and also an appeal to God's promise. We find both the prayer and the promise throughout the Old Testament.

God 'remembers' Noah and all the animals on the ark and delivers them from the flood (Genesis 8:1).

God 'remembers' the childless Rachel, and she conceives and gives birth to Joseph (Genesis 30:22-24).

God hears the cries of the Israelites in Egypt, remembers the covenant made with Abraham, and delivers them from slavery (Exodus 2:23-25)."

The psalmist writes:
"Be mindful of your mercy, O Lord, and of your steadfast love…
Do not remember the sins of my youth or my transgressions;
according to Your steadfast love remember me,
for Your goodness' sake, O Lord!" – Psalm 25:6-7

Jesus' response to the criminal's request is immediate:
"Truly I tell you, today you will be with me in paradise."

Paradise—the fulfillment of God's kingdom, where one is with Christ in the presence of God.
At the moment of his confession, the criminal began eternity with Jesus.
He was no longer defined by his past crimes. Jesus gave him peace and assurance.

The kingdom of God, salvation, and living in God's presence begin today for those who place their trust in Jesus. This is what Jesus meant when He said:

"I have come that they may have life, and have it to the full." – John 10:10

"I am the resurrection and the life." – John 11:25

Theologian John Wesley wrote:
"…It is not a blessing which lies on the other side of death… It is not something at a distance: it is a present thing, a blessing, which, through the free mercy of God, ye are now in possession of."

To what extent do you live as though you are already experiencing the blessing of salvation?

"Today, you will be with me in paradise."

16

Jesus assured the second criminal that **today**, his sins were forgiven.

Today, he could live in the reality of God's kingdom that would never end.

Today, he was set free.

This promise was not just for the man on the cross beside Jesus.

It is for you and me. It is for the whole world.

And now, as His disciples, we are called to share this message—not just with words, but through the way we live.

Take a moment to sit with the Lord.

Where will you show others a glimpse of God's kingdom this week?

Close your time in prayer, thanking Jesus for the blessings of salvation that begins **today**—and asking Him to help you live fully in the reality of what you have in His love.

Day 4: Here is Your Mother

"Woman, here is your son'... 'Here is your mother." –
John 19:26-27

Read: John 19:1-27

The Gospels of Matthew, Mark, and Luke refer to Jesus'
mother as Mary, yet John's Gospel never mentions her by
name. Instead, he refers to her only as **"the mother of
Jesus."**
Surely, John knew her name.
Why do you think he chose to refer to her only in this way?

Likewise, "the disciple whom Jesus loved" is also left
unnamed.
But in His final words, Jesus calls these two into a new family
relationship.
John, who does not reference either "mother" or "son" by
name, seems to be highlighting something significant.
What do you think is the deeper meaning behind this new
family connection?
What might John want his readers to understand?

Go back to the beginning of John's Gospel:

*"In the beginning was the Word, and the Word was with God, and the
Word was God. He was with God in the beginning. Through him all
things were made; without him nothing was made that has been made. In
him was life, and that life was the light of all mankind. The light shines
in the darkness, and the darkness has not overcome it." –* John 1:1-5

"Yet to all who did receive him, to those who believed in his name, he gave the right to become children of God—children born not of natural descent, nor of human decision or a husband's will, but born of God." – John 1:12-13

Jesus became flesh, lived among us, and endured the shame and horror of the cross so that we could be born again—not just in the image of God, but as children of God.
French theologian Pierre Teilhard de Chardin described this transformation as moving from *"human beings having a spiritual experience to spiritual beings having a human experience."*

Read: Luke 8:19-21

"Now Jesus' mother and brothers came to see him, but they were not able to get near him because of the crowd. Someone told him, 'Your mother and brothers are standing outside, wanting to see you.'
He replied, 'My mother and brothers are those who hear God's word and put it into practice.'" – Luke 8:19-21

At first glance, Jesus' response might seem shocking—even disrespectful.
How do you think the people in the crowd perceived His words?
How do you think His own family felt?

What was Jesus saying about the true definition of family?

Have you ever experienced a relationship with someone outside of your biological family that reshaped your understanding of what it means to be family?
What was your experience?

Notice that Jesus defines family by action—not just by belief.

"My mother and brothers are those who hear God's word and put it into practice."

At the cross, Jesus doesn't merely instruct the beloved disciple to **care** for His mother.
He says, **"Here is your mother."**

John then writes:
"From that time on, this disciple took her into his home." – John 19:27

John does not say the disciple simply agreed to help Mary—he says he took her in as family.
What does John want us to understand about the disciple's response?

How does this challenge or inspire your own call to discipleship?
Is there an area in your life where you need to live more fully into your calling to care for the members of your heavenly family?

Through Christ's resurrection power, we are not only redeemed but transformed. What may seem broken beyond repair, Jesus can restore. He takes what appears to be lost and turns it into something beautiful. This is our hope—His promise. Lean in. Listen. Love one another as true family in Christ.

Take time to sit with the Lord. Where is He calling you to lean in? Who in your life needs to experience the love of God's family through you today? Close your time in prayer, asking God to help you live as a true child of His kingdom, embracing those around you as family in Christ.

Day 5: I am Thirsty

"I am thirsty." – John 19:28

Read: John 17

Can you sense Jesus praying for you personally in this passage?

"Jesus knew that his mission was now finished, and to fulfill Scripture he said, 'I am thirsty.' A jar of sour wine was sitting there, so they soaked a sponge in it, put it on a hyssop branch, and held it up to his lips. When Jesus had tasted it, he said, 'It is finished!' Then he bowed his head and gave up his spirit." – John 19:28-30

It can be easy to focus so much on Jesus' divinity that we forget He was also fully human.

John's Gospel makes Jesus' divine nature clear:
"In the beginning was the Word, and the Word was with God, and the Word was God. He was with God in the beginning. Through him all things were made; without him nothing was made that has been made." – John 1:1-3

Consider some of Jesus' **"I am"** statements:

"I tell you the truth, before Abraham was even born, I am."
– John 8:58

"I am the way, the truth, and the life. No one can come to the Father except through me." – John 14:6

"I am the gate for the sheep… I am the good shepherd. The good shepherd lays down his life for the sheep." – John 10:7-11

"I am the resurrection and the life. The one who believes in me will live, even though they die." – John 11:25-26

Yet in His final moments on the cross, Jesus' last **"I am"** statement is different.

"I am thirsty."

At this moment, John highlights Jesus' full humanity—His human needs and suffering.

Matthew records that before Jesus was crucified,
"they offered Jesus wine to drink, mixed with gall; but after tasting it, he refused to drink it." – Matthew 27:34

Mark describes the drink as wine mixed with myrrh.
The drink offered to Jesus was a cheap vinegar wine, mixed with a drug to dull the senses—a customary Roman practice to numb the pain of crucifixion.

But Jesus refused it.
He chose to fully experience the suffering of the cross, facing death with a clear mind, bearing the full weight of the world's sin.
Finally, as He neared death, He expressed His thirst.
John tells us this was "so that Scripture would be fulfilled."

Read: Psalm 69:19-21

By expressing His thirst, Jesus was revealing not only His physical pain but also His full participation in human suffering.
He understands your pain.
He understands your trials.
He understands your suffering—because He lived it.

And because you are a child of God, He walks through your trials with you.
You are not alone.

The one who offers living water—water that leads to eternal life—is thirsty.
He thirsts physically due to blood loss and extreme dehydration from the cross.
And spiritually, He drinks the bitter cup of death to save us from sin.

"Whoever drinks the water I give them will never thirst. Indeed, the water I give them will become in them a spring of water welling up to eternal life." – John 4:14

Only Jesus can satisfy our deepest desires.
Yet, how often do we seek to quench our spiritual thirst elsewhere?
Where in your life have you tried to satisfy your deepest needs with something other than Christ?

And in your journey with the Lord, what thirsts has He already quenched?

Jesus calls us not only to receive His living water but to pour it out for others.

"Out of the believer's heart shall flow rivers of living water."
– John 7:38

When we allow Jesus' living water to fill us, it doesn't just satisfy us—it flows through us to bless others.
Who in your life needs to experience this living water?
How will you be Jesus' hands and feet this week?

Close your time in prayer, asking Jesus to fill your soul with His living water and to help you share His love with those who thirst. Pray that you may see needs around you that you might not have otherwise noticed and that God will work through you to help, support, and bless others. Surrender your own thirst to Him, trusting that as He fills you, He will also equip you to be a source of hope, encouragement, and light to those He places in your path

Week 2

Devotionals

Day 1: Into Your Hands I Commit My Spirit

"Father, into your hands I commit my spirit." - Luke 23:46

Are there places where you feel closest to God? Are there places where you cannot help but notice His presence? Perhaps you feel this way while out in nature, seeing the handiwork of His creation. Maybe it happens while standing on the shore, looking out at the vastness of the ocean, or gazing at the stars on a clear night.

Are there places where God's presence just feels stronger to you?

Read: Luke 23:44-49

As you read the description of Jesus' crucifixion, what do you notice about God's presence in this scene? What stands out to you? What adjectives would you use to describe it?

Do you have any favorite Bible verses that you turn to in times of distress? Are there any verses that you have memorized or return to again and again when you are fearful, upset, discouraged, or anxious?

What are they?

How is it helpful to turn these scriptures into prayers, guiding your conversation with God when you are distressed, anxious, or troubled?

It is no surprise that some of Jesus' last words on the cross were prayers from the Psalms.

Read: Psalm 31:1-5

We hear Jesus' words in one line of this psalm, but He knew the psalm in its entirety.

Read: Psalm 31:9-13

How do the words reflect His situation on the cross?

Jot down the words or phrases that stand out to you.

Like so many psalms that cry out to the Lord in anguish and distress, this psalm ends with a note of hope and praise.

Read: Psalm 31:21-24

Are you currently facing any situation, trouble, or hardship where you need to feel God's kindness? Is there something in your heart right now that needs reassurance that your cries are being heard by God? Where do you need His courage and strength?

"Be of good courage, and He shall strengthen your heart, all you who hope in the Lord." – Psalm 31:24

Do you think you fully entrust your life to the Lord? Do you trust Him with everything—your past, your present, and your future? What about your plans, your hopes, and your fears? You may want to trust Him completely, but do you actually live and walk in that trust?

What, if anything, holds you back from fully entrusting everything to God?

"But as for me, I trust in You, O Lord; I say, 'You are my God.' My times are in Your hand." – Psalm 31:14-15

Imagine if you committed to praying every day, "Father, into your hands I commit my spirit" or "Father, into your hands I commit my life." If you began each day with that prayer, how might your week be different? Could it help you more fully put your trust in the Lord? Could it give you more courage or keep you from worrying about things outside of your control?

"Into your hands I commit my spirit" are not just words to die by. These are powerful words to live by. They are words that teach us how to trust, how to surrender, and how to walk in peace.

Read: Matthew 6:25-34

How could praying this prayer help you live out Jesus' teaching in the book of Matthew?

Can you pray this prayer each day this week?

"Lord, God, into your hands I commit my life. Into your hands I commit this day. I don't know what this day will hold, but I know You, and Your hands hold each one of my days."

Jesus is speaking to us from the cross. He is sharing with us a trust that withstands any trial, assurance that God is in control, and peace that surpasses all understanding.

Will you receive it?

Day 2: Palm Sunday

Jesus prepares His disciples for His death as the day draws near.

Read: Luke 18:31-33

What is Jesus trying to tell His disciples in these verses? Do they understand Him?

Jesus is warning the disciples that He must go to Jerusalem, suffer, and be killed. He must do this to fulfill the Scriptures and the words of the prophets.

"Then he said to the crowd, 'If any of you wants to be my follower, you must give up your own way, take up your cross daily, and follow me.'" – Luke 9:23

If we are to sincerely follow Christ and be His disciples, we too must take up our crosses and follow after Him.
What does this mean to you?

Read: Luke 19:33-39

Jesus enters Jerusalem in what may seem like an unusual way, yet the crowd seems to recognize exactly what is happening. How did the Pharisees respond to this scene? Why?

"Rejoice, O people of Zion!
Shout in triumph, O people of Jerusalem!
Look, your king is coming to you.
He is righteous and victorious,

yet he is humble, riding on a donkey—
riding on a donkey's colt." – Zechariah 9:9

This verse prophesied the coming of a king, righteous and victorious, yet lowly and riding on a donkey.
This prophecy was fulfilled when Jesus entered Jerusalem on a donkey.

Read: Matthew 21:1-11

"A very large crowd spread their cloaks on the road, while others cut branches from the trees and spread them on the road."

All four Gospels record Jesus' triumphant entry into Jerusalem (Matthew 21:1-11, Mark 11:1-11, Luke 19:28-34, and John 12:12-15).

The crowd spread palm branches and cloaks on the road, waving them as they celebrated Jesus. They shouted:
"Hosanna to the Son of David!
Blessed is He who comes in the name of the Lord!
Hosanna in the highest!"

Their words and actions were rich in meaning. Laying down cloaks and branches was an act of enthronement, a recognition of royalty.

"They quickly took their cloaks and spread them under him on the bare steps. Then they blew the trumpet and shouted, 'Jehu is king!'" – 2 Kings 9:13

For generations, the Jewish people had been waiting for the Messiah. As Jesus entered Jerusalem, the crowd not only mirrored the actions from Jehu's coronation in 2 Kings, but also quoted Psalm 118:

"Blessed is he who comes in the name of the Lord.
From the house of the Lord we bless you." – Psalm 118:26

The crowd treated Jesus as their long-awaited king.
What did they expect Him to do next?

Many people were disappointed when Jesus did not fulfill
their expectations.
Have you ever known someone who was disappointed when
God didn't meet their expectations?

Have you ever felt disappointed when God didn't answer
your prayers in the way you had hoped?

This week before Easter is known as Passion Week. The
Latin root for the word "passion" is *passio* or *pati*,
meaning suffering.
Jesus came as a suffering servant.

"He was despised and rejected by mankind,
a man of suffering, and familiar with pain.
Like one from whom people hide their faces
he was despised, and we held him in low esteem.
Surely he took up our pain
and bore our suffering,
yet we considered him punished by God,
stricken by him, and afflicted.
But he was pierced for our transgressions,
he was crushed for our iniquities;
the punishment that brought us peace was on him,
and by his wounds we are healed." – Isaiah 53:3-5

Yet Jesus is also the King of Kings.

"He is clothed in a robe dipped in blood, and the name by which he is called is The Word of God. . . . On his robe and on his thigh he has a name written, King of kings and Lord of lords." – Revelation 19:13,16

Has your view of Jesus—suffering servant or triumphant king—varied throughout your life?
How do different seasons of life, trials, or circumstances shape the way you relate to these two images of Jesus?

What can you do this week to stay focused on the true meaning of Easter?
Conclude your time in prayer, asking God to prepare your heart for this Holy Week. Reflect on how He may be speaking to you through this passage. Is He calling you to surrender your expectations, trust in His greater plan, or embrace Him more fully as both the suffering servant and triumphant King? Take a moment to listen and respond to His voice today.

Day 3: The Last Supper

Read: John 13:1-17

Why was it important for Jesus to wash the disciples' feet?

Certainly, Jesus was teaching humility and service toward others. He was setting an example for us to follow. But what other meaning might we discover from this encounter?

Peter was focused on the physical act being performed, appalled at the thought of his Lord serving him in such a way. *"You do not realize now what I am doing, but later you will understand."* And then, *"If I do not wash you, you have no part with Me."*

Eventually, Scripture would be opened more fully to the disciples, revealing how every act of Christ fulfilled what had been written about Him.
Let's consider the meaning of this washing as foretold in Scripture:

"Wash me clean from my guilt. Purify me from my sin." – Psalm 51:2

"Purify me from my sins, and I will be clean; wash me, and I will be whiter than snow." – Psalm 51:7

"Then I will sprinkle clean water on you, and you will be clean. Your filth will be washed away, and you will no longer worship idols." – Ezekiel 36:25

"What are you waiting for? Get up and be baptized. Have your sins washed away by calling on the name of the Lord." – Acts 22:16

"But you were cleansed; you were made holy; you were made right with God by calling on the name of the Lord Jesus Christ and by the Spirit of our God." – 1 Corinthians 6:11

"Let us go right into the presence of God with sincere hearts fully trusting Him. For our guilty consciences have been sprinkled with Christ's blood to make us clean, and our bodies have been washed with pure water." – Hebrews 10:22

Unless our sins are washed away, we can have no part with Jesus.
Even at this late stage in their time with Christ, the disciples still did not fully grasp His mission. They continued to seek an earthly kingdom, failing to realize that His kingdom was spiritual. This simple act of washing their feet was to show that unless they were cleansed of their sins, they could not inherit the kingdom of God. The message of repentance and forgiveness was at the very heart of Christ's teachings.

Max Lucado writes in *He Chose the Nails*:
"We can't be more saved than we were the day we accepted Christ's sacrifice on the cross and received salvation, but we can grow in that salvation."

Paul describes this growth in 2 Corinthians 3:18:
"And the Lord—who is Spirit—makes us more and more like him as we are changed into his glorious image."

The Message translation puts it this way:
"And so we are transfigured much like the Messiah, our lives gradually becoming brighter and more beautiful as God enters our lives and we become like Him."

The word "changed" in this verse comes from the same root as the English word metamorphosis—a complete transformation, like a caterpillar becoming a butterfly.
This change is not instantaneous; it is gradual growth.

How have you seen a gradual metamorphosis in your own life as a Christian?

How does the thought of this kind of transformation bring you hope?

How would you like to see your life become brighter and more beautiful as you walk with the Lord?

Jesus did not say, *"Now that I, your Lord and Teacher, have washed your feet, you also should wash others' feet."* Instead, He said: *"You also should wash one another's feet."*

What does He mean by "one another"?

Jesus calls us to serve others, but He also calls us to receive love and service from others. Our washing is mutual. We should humbly serve, but we should also humbly receive love from others in Jesus' name.

Which is more difficult for you—serving others or receiving service and sacrifice from others? Why?

Continue reading about the Last Supper.

Read: Luke 22:1-38

Here we read about Judas' betrayal of Jesus. We are told that Judas betrayed Him for only thirty pieces of silver (Matthew 26:15). Even in Jesus' day, this was not a large sum of money. Judas' heart was bought out for an embarrassingly small amount.
We, too, often betray God for things that are fleeting and insignificant.

What are some of the things you choose **over God**?
How do you betray Jesus with your words or by your lifestyle?
What behavior betrays your relationship with Jesus that you need to ask God to help you change?

Jesus, our Passover Lamb, delivers believers from the bondage of sin through His atoning work on the cross. He fulfills the promise of the new covenant found in Jeremiah 31:31-34:

"The day is coming," says the Lord, "when I will make a new covenant with the people of Israel and Judah. This covenant will not be like the one I made with their ancestors when I took them by the hand and brought them out of the land of Egypt. They broke that covenant, though I loved them as a husband loves his wife," says the Lord.
"But this is the new covenant I will make with the people of Israel after those days," says the Lord. "I will put my instructions deep within them, and I will write them on their hearts. I will be their God, and they will be my people. And they will not need to teach their neighbors, nor will they need to teach their relatives, saying, 'You should know the Lord.' For everyone, from the least to the greatest, will know me already," says the Lord. "And I will forgive their wickedness, and I will never again remember their sins."

You are the sick that Jesus came to heal.
You are the lost that Jesus came to find.
You are the sinner that Jesus came to save.

"This is my body, given for you."
Close your time in prayer and listen for what Jesus may be saying to you today.

Day 4: The Veil Was Torn

Read: Matthew 27

"And behold, the veil of the temple was torn in two from top to bottom." – Matthew 27:51

This veil was the inner veil before the Holy of Holies. It was made of blue, purple, and scarlet yarn and finely twisted linen, with cherubim woven into it by a skilled craftsman.

"Make a curtain of blue, purple and scarlet yarn and finely twisted linen, with cherubim woven into it by a skilled worker." – Exodus 26:31

This veil separated the Holy Place from the Holy of Holies, where God's presence was said to rest and where the Ark of the Covenant was kept. Only the High Priest could enter this Most Holy Place, and even then, only once a year on the Day of Atonement to make atonement for the sins of Israel.

The veil marked the separation between God's holiness and sinful humanity. Worshipers under the old covenant were restricted in their access to God. Only a high priest who was ritually pure and without defect could approach God without being put to death.

When Jesus died, this barrier was removed.

"In speaking of a new covenant, he makes the first one obsolete. And what is becoming obsolete and growing old is ready to vanish away." – Hebrews 8:13

The tearing of the veil marked the beginning of a new covenant. No longer would access to God be restricted. Because of Christ's death, all believers may boldly come before God's throne.

Notice the power for this miracle came *during* the sacrifice. When Jesus gave up His spirit, the veil was torn. The veil was torn when Jesus was on the cross, not three days later when He rose from the dead.

"Therefore, brothers and sisters, since we have confidence to enter the Most Holy Place by the blood of Jesus, by a new and living way opened for us through the curtain, that is, his body…" – Hebrews 10:19-20

Jesus invites us into His Father's presence. What once separated us from God has been removed.

There may be no physical veil in the temple today, but often we allow a veil to remain in our hearts—things that prevent us from fully stepping into God's presence.

Guilt, shame, past regrets, an ongoing sin we ignore, an inability to trust—these can all create barriers between us and our loving Father.

What are the barriers in your life that keep you from fully entering into God's presence?

Guilt and shame can become a curtain of the heart, causing us to hide from God's presence.

When faced with guilt, self-disappointment, or other struggles, do any of these statements describe why you may be hiding behind a veil?

- I'm hiding from what I imagine is God's anger or disapproval.
- I'm keeping my distance from God until I can get my act together.
- I'm shielding myself from my own shame.
- I can't bring myself to confess and face my failure.
- I feel unable to make peace or seek forgiveness from others.
- I don't know if I can make necessary changes.

Remember: God isn't angry with you. He has already dealt with your mistakes. He has already dealt with your sin. He has already forgiven you, and He invites you into His presence.

Pastor and author Eugene Peterson writes:

"No one was permitted into the Holy of Holies except the High Priest, and then only once a year. The holy and the profane were strictly separated... And so the shock is nothing less than seismic to be told that the first thing that happened when Jesus died on the cross was that 'the curtain of the temple was torn in two, from top to bottom.'

What happened? The Holy Place is now Every Place. The Holy One of God is contemporary with us. His time is our time. There is no more separation between there and here, then and now, sacred and secular... The death of Jesus on the cross opens up a 'new and living way' by which we can live an integrated life."

To live an integrated life means that every part of life becomes whole—no longer separated into compartments.

Every place becomes a holy place.

There are no places off-limits to God's presence.

Even our sin, shame, and guilt are invited behind the veil.

Yet it is easy to fall into compartmentalized thinking—dividing life into what feels holy and what feels secular.

Do you ever compartmentalize your life with any of these thoughts?

- God is in **holy places** but not in **every place**.
- I've seen God at work in **some areas of my life** but not in **all areas**.
- God was present in **past circumstances**, but I'm not sure He is present now.
- I can come before God in **church, my quiet time, or Bible study**, but not when I feel sinful, angry, or unworthy.

God has given you full access to His presence.

Are you making the most of this incredible gift?

Conclude your time in prayer, asking God to remove any veils in your heart that keep you from fully stepping into His presence. Reflect on what He may be speaking to you today. What is He inviting you to surrender? Where is He calling you to walk in freedom?

Day 5: He Is Risen!

He is risen indeed!

We experience the journey of Jesus' resurrection over three days, each reflecting different seasons in our own lives. Friday is a day of fear, pain, and heartache. Saturday brings discouragement and hopelessness. But Sunday is a day of freedom and joy. Throughout life, we will face all three—times of suffering, times of waiting, and times of victory.
We will experience all of these "days" repeatedly in our lives. We will face fear and grief, disillusionment and discouragement, and overwhelming joy and peace.

How should we handle the "Fridays" of life—when we face fear, anxiety, or grief?

We should respond as Jesus did—seeking support from friends and turning to God in prayer.

Read: Matthew 26:36-39

In His time of greatest need, Jesus brought His disciples with Him to Gethsemane to pray. He did not choose to face His darkest hour alone.

When you experience fear, anxiety, grief, or darkness, this is the time to seek support.
Jesus drew His friends close and told them how He was feeling.

Do you need to reach out to someone for support?
Do you need to draw someone close and say, *"I'm anxious. I'm struggling right now"*?
Or maybe *you* need to be that support for someone else.

"Carry each other's burdens, and in this way you will fulfill the law of Christ." – Galatians 6:2

Jesus was about to face the ultimate physical pain. Emotionally, He was about to experience ridicule, betrayal, humiliation, shame, and disgrace. Spiritually, He was preparing to take on the guilt of every sin ever committed. In the face of this suffering, He surrounded Himself with those closest to Him, and then He fell before the Father in prayer.

"Going a little farther, he fell to the ground and prayed that if possible the hour might pass from him. 'Abba, Father,' he said, 'everything is possible for you. Take this cup from me. Yet not what I will, but what you will.'" – Mark 14:35-36

When facing fear, grief, or pain, we can follow Jesus' example in prayer.

First, He affirmed God's power: *"Everything is possible for you."* He recognized that God was in control and sovereign over all things. In the same way, we are called to acknowledge God's supremacy, His greatness, and His power, trusting that all things will unfold according to His perfect plan.

Next, He expressed His deep and true desires: *"Take this cup from me."* Jesus did not shy away from His anguish. He openly admitted His suffering, the weight of what was to come, and the pain He did not want to endure. In our own moments of distress, we, too, are invited to come before God with

46

complete honesty—laying our fears, worries, and burdens at His feet. He desires our raw, unfiltered prayers, not just polished words.

Finally, He surrendered to the Father's will: *"Yet not what I will, but what you will."* This is the moment of deepest trust—the choice to believe that God's ways are higher than ours. It is in these moments that we place trust before fear, knowing that even when we don't feel His presence, He is walking beside us. Even when we don't see His plan, He is working all things together for good.

The "Saturdays" of life are filled with confusion, disillusionment, and hopelessness.

Read: Matthew 27:57-61

For Jesus' followers, it seemed as if life had fallen apart. They were grief-stricken, hopeless, and discouraged.

"And Mary Magdalene was there, and the other Mary, sitting opposite the tomb."

Imagine being one of these women, sitting and watching.
What is going through your mind?
What is going through your heart?

How should we respond to the "Saturdays" of life?

When faith is shaken, when we feel sorrow, confusion, or grief, it can be easy to turn away from God.

Even Jesus' own disciples abandoned Him in fear.

"At that point, all the disciples abandoned Jesus and ran away." – Matthew 26:56

Have you ever deserted God out of confusion, fear, or grief?

Rather than running away from God, we need to run into His arms and cling to His promises:

- **God sees you.**
- **God knows you.**
- **God loves you.**
- **God is close to you.**
- **God wants what's best for you.**
- **God can create good from bad.**
- **God is with you.**
- **God is your Savior.**
- **God will turn despair, grief, and death into praise and glory.**

"When you go through deep waters and great trouble, I will be with you. When you go through rivers of difficulty, you will not drown! When you walk through the fire of oppression, you will not be burned up—the flames will not consume you. For I am the Lord your God, your Savior." – Isaiah 43:2-3

"To those who mourn, He will give a crown of beauty for ashes, a joyous blessing instead of mourning, festive praise instead of despair." – Isaiah 61:3

If you hold onto the promises of God, you will inevitably make it to Sunday—the day of rejoicing and freedom.

Jesus said, "The truth will set you free."
And He also said, "I am the truth, the way, and the life."
To reach the joy and freedom of the "Sundays" of life, we need to rely on the power of Jesus.

Read: John 20:15-21

You can move past the Fridays and Saturdays of life.
You can overcome the darkest days by seeking the Lord, remembering His promises, and relying on the power of Jesus.
Because He lives, your life is blessed, and your eternity is secure.

And because of you, others' lives will be blessed, and eternities will be secure as well.

"I pray that you will begin to understand how incredibly great His power is to help those who believe in Him. It is that same mighty power that raised Christ from the dead..." – Ephesians 1:19-20

Happy Easter, my dear friend in Christ!
He is risen indeed!

Bonus Leader Guide

Come to the Cross

Leader Guide Contents

WELCOME

Welcome to the *Come to the Cross* Leader Guide. This guide is designed to help you lead meaningful discussions and foster deep connections within your small group as you journey through the devotionals.

Easter is the foundation of our faith—the moment in history that changed everything. This study invites us to walk alongside Jesus in His final days, witness His suffering, hear His last words, and rejoice in His victory over death. Each devotional provides an opportunity to reflect on the power of the cross, the depth of Christ's love, and the hope of the resurrection.

Throughout this study, your group will experience the weight of Good Friday, the silence of Saturday, and the joy of Resurrection Sunday. You will discuss Jesus' radical forgiveness, His suffering, His ultimate sacrifice, and the invitation He offers us into eternal life.

Each session is an opportunity to not only grow in knowledge but to experience deep, personal connection with the Lord as you reflect on how Christ's death and resurrection impact your own life.

As you lead this small group, know that God is at work. He is moving in the hearts of those who are gathered. This is a time to encourage one another, support one another, and walk together in faith. It is a time to set aside distractions, fears, and doubts, and to draw closer to the cross—to Jesus Himself.

Remember, God is speaking—to you and through you. As you use this guide, trust that the Lord will work in your life and in the lives of those in your group. Together, you will reflect on the suffering and sacrifice of Jesus, the meaning of the cross, and the hope of resurrection.

I'm honored to walk through this journey with you and look forward to seeing how God moves in your life and in the lives of those in your group.
Let's begin.

Leading Your Group

As you begin the journey of leading a small group through *Come to the Cross*, you have **two options** for structuring your discussions. You may choose to focus solely on the Easter devotionals, or you can pair this Leader Guide with **SoulStrength Fit's corresponding faith-based fitness program**, designed to integrate scripture, reflection, and and exercise as a continuation of your time with God. Regardless of your choice, this Leader Guide is designed to equip you with the tools necessary to facilitate meaningful discussions, foster deeper connections, and support others in their walk with the Lord.

Structure of This Leader Guide

This guide is designed to be used over **two meetings**:

1. **Meeting One:** Discuss reflections from **Week 1** of the devotionals, focusing on Jesus' final words and the depth of His sacrifice.
2. **Meeting Two:** Discuss reflections from **Week 2**, journeying through Jesus' death, the torn veil, and the ultimate victory of His resurrection.

Each meeting provides a structured framework to encourage reflection, personal insight, and group support. This approach emphasizes building a strong community, deepening relationships, and growing in faith as your group walks through the powerful events of Holy Week.

Option 1: Using *Come to the Cross* Alone

If your group is focusing exclusively on the devotionals, this Leader Guide provides a framework for a two-week small group experience. Each session is designed to help members reflect on Jesus' sacrifice and resurrection, share personal insights, and support one another as they draw closer to the heart of God.

This approach fosters spiritual growth, meaningful discussion, and deeper connections, allowing participants to truly absorb the significance of Jesus' final words and His triumph over the grave.

Option 2: Pairing with SoulStrength Fit's

Come to the Cross Faith-Based Fitness Program

For a complete **mind-body-spirit experience**, consider pairing the *Come to the Cross* devotionals with **SoulStrength Fit's Come to the Cross Faith-Based Fitness Program**. This option enhances your group's experience by integrating exercise, prayer, and Christ-centered reflection into two weeks of workouts

This program includes:

- **Faith-based workouts** that correspond with the Easter devotionals, combining exercise with scripture reflection.
- **An opportunity to use exercise as worship**, engaging both body and spirit in honoring Christ.
- **A space for accountability and encouragement**, strengthening both faith and fitness through shared commitment.

This Leader Guide provides all the tools needed to facilitate two weekly meetings, offering your group a space to come together, reflect, and grow in faith while also incorporating a physical aspect to their spiritual journey. To learn more or sign up, visit **www.soulstrengthfit.com**.

Getting Started

Whether you choose to focus on the devotionals alone or incorporate the faith-based fitness program as a way to deepen your connection with God, this Leader Guide will help you lead your group through a beautiful and personal Easter study. Select the option that best fits your group's needs and prepare to guide them toward a deeper understanding of Jesus' sacrifice, His victory over death, and what that means for our lives today.

Tips for Leading Your Group

Creating a **supportive and engaging small group environment** is essential to the success of your meetings. Start by **encouraging participation and fostering a space of openness and connection.**

- **Create a welcoming atmosphere** where members feel comfortable sharing their reflections, struggles, and victories.
- **Ask questions with warmth and genuine interest**, and listen attentively to responses.
- **Encourage vulnerability and honesty** while allowing space for those who may take longer to open up.
- **Let the discussion flow naturally**—you don't have to get through every question, and it's okay to spend more time on the topics that resonate deeply.

As a leader, you are a guide, not an expert. Feel free to reword questions or adjust discussions as needed for your group. If questions arise that you don't have answers to, it's perfectly fine to say, *"I'm not sure about that, but let's explore it together."* This can be an opportunity for deeper discussion and learning as a group.

Above all, trust that God will work through your discussions. Let Him lead you as you walk alongside others in discovering the power of the cross and the joy of resurrection.

Session 1

Welcome & Opening Prayer

Start the meeting by welcoming everyone and opening with prayer. Encourage members to pray for **guidance, wisdom, and an open heart** as they reflect on Jesus' sacrifice and resurrection.

Introductions & Building Community

Encourage each member to introduce themselves. Here are some questions to help build community and foster connection:

- What brought you to this group, and what do you hope to gain from it?
- What is one thing you're passionate about outside of your faith?
- What is a favorite Bible verse or story that has impacted your life?
- What's one area of your life where you're seeking to grow spiritually?

Discussion Questions

You are forgiven. You are reconciled with God. You are whole and holy in His presence.

Kelly writes:
"You are not defined by your worst mistakes. Because of Jesus, you stand before God holy and pure. You are growing into the image of Christ every day. Transformation takes time. Often, we don't notice the changes happening in us."

- Reflecting on your faith journey, what is one **gradual but significant change** you have experienced?
- How can this encourage you in the areas of your life where change still feels slow?

"Eloi, Eloi, lema sabachthani?" (which means "My God, my God, why have you forsaken me?")

What a deep, heartfelt cry—Jesus expressing His feeling of being forsaken by God.

- Have you ever **felt forsaken by God**?
- Have you ever felt forgotten, abandoned, or unheard?
- Is there a time when you felt God was far away?

"Today, you will be with me in paradise."

Kelly writes that Jesus assured the second criminal that today, his sins were forgiven. Today, he could live in the reality of God's kingdom that would never end. Today, he was set free. This promise was not just for the man on the cross beside Jesus—it is for you and me.

- To what extent do you live as though you are **already experiencing the blessing of salvation?**
- How can you **daily experience** the blessings that come through your faith and relationship with Jesus, and what might sometimes **prevent** you from fully embracing those blessings?

"My mother and brothers are those who hear God's word and put it into practice."

Notice that **Jesus defines family by action—not just by belief.**

- How does this **challenge or inspire** your own call to discipleship?
- Is there an area in your life where you need to live more fully into your calling to care for the members of your heavenly family?

"Whoever drinks the water I give them will never thirst. Indeed, the water I give them will become in them a spring of water welling up to eternal life." – John 4:14

Only Jesus can **satisfy our deepest desires.**

- Yet, how often do we seek to quench our spiritual thirst elsewhere?
- Where in your life have you **tried to satisfy your deepest needs** with something other than Christ?

Jesus calls us not only to receive His living water but to pour it out for others.

"Out of the believer's heart shall flow rivers of living water." – John 7:38

When we allow **Jesus' living water to fill us**, it doesn't just satisfy us—it **flows through us to bless others**.

- Who in your life **needs to experience this living water?**
- How will you **be Jesus' hands and feet** this week?

Accountability Check-In

(If pairing with the SoulStrength Fit Workout Program)

- Did you **complete your workouts** this week? What helped you stay on track, or what challenges made it difficult?
- How did you feel about your **nutrition and eating habits** this week? Share a specific example of a day when you felt **aligned with your goals** or a time when it was challenging to stay on track.

Encourage group members to **support one another**, share any victories or struggles, and offer **practical encouragement and accountability**.

Closing Prayer & Prayer Requests

Invite each member to share a personal prayer request. Close in prayer, asking God to make His presence abundantly clear in the week ahead and to deepen each person's understanding of His love, grace, and sacrifice.

Looking Ahead

In the next session, members will discuss reflections from **Week 2** of the devotionals, focusing on Jesus' death, the torn veil, and the victory of His resurrection. Encourage everyone to take notes on their experiences and any insights God reveals to them throughout the week.

Session 2

Welcome & Opening Prayer

Start the meeting by welcoming everyone and opening with prayer. Encourage members to pray for **wisdom, openness, and a deeper connection with God** as they reflect on Jesus' sacrifice and resurrection.

Discussion Questions

Scriptures for Strength in Difficult Times

- Do you have any favorite Bible verses that you turn to in times of distress?
- Are there any verses that you have memorized or return to again and again when you are fearful, upset, discouraged, or anxious?

Read: **Psalm 31:21-24**

- Are you currently facing any situation, trouble, or hardship in which you need to feel God's kindness?
- Is there something in your heart right now where you need to feel that your cries are being heard by God?
- Where do you need His courage and strength?

Taking Up Your Cross

"Then he said to the crowd, 'If any of you wants to be my follower, you must give up your own way, take up your cross daily, and follow me.'" – Luke 9:23

- If we are to **sincerely follow Christ**, we too must take up our crosses and follow after Him.
- What does this **mean to you**?

Serving & Receiving in Christ's Love

Jesus did not say, "Now that I, your Lord and Teacher, have washed your feet, you also should wash others' feet." But rather, He said, **"You also should wash one another's feet."**

- What does He mean by **"one another"**?
- Jesus calls us not only to serve but also to humbly receive love, service, and sacrifice from others. Which is more difficult for you?
  - Humbly **serving others**?
  - Or **receiving service and sacrifice** from others?
  - Why?

Recognizing Betrayal in Our Own Lives

We read about Judas' betrayal of Jesus. He sold out his Lord for only 30 pieces of silver (Matthew 26:15). Even in Jesus' day, this wasn't much money. Judas' heart was bought out for an embarrassingly small amount.

- We often betray God for things that are fleeting and insignificant. What are some of those things we choose **every day over God?**
- How do you betray Jesus with your **words or by your lifestyle?**
- What **behavior that betrays your relationship with Jesus** will you ask God to help you change?

The Veil Was Torn – A New Invitation

"And behold, the veil of the temple was torn in two from top to bottom." – Matthew 27:51

- Jesus invites us into His Father's presence. What once separated us from God has been removed.
- There may be no **physical veil**, but often we **put up a veil in our hearts.**
  - A **guilty conscience**
  - An **ongoing sin ignored**
  - An **inability to let go of past hurts or regrets**
  - An **inability to fully trust God**
- What barriers have you put up between yourself and God?

The "Fridays," "Saturdays," and "Sundays" of Life

Kelly writes that **Jesus' resurrection took place over the course of three days:**

- **Friday was a day of fear, pain, and heartache.**
- **Saturday was a day of discouragement and hopelessness.**

- **Sunday was a day of freedom and joy.**

We all experience these **three types of days in life**.

Responding to the "Fridays" of Life

- When we experience **the "Fridays" of life—fear, pain, and grief**—we should respond as Jesus did.
- We should seek support from friends, and we should turn to God in prayer.
- Do you need to **reach out to someone for support**?
- Do you need to **draw someone close** and let them know, "I'm anxious; I'm afraid"?
- Or maybe you need to **be there for someone else** right now.

Responding to the "Saturdays" of Life

"How should we respond to the "Saturdays" of life?"

- When your faith is shaken, when you're **filled with sorrow, confusion, or grief**, it can be easy to turn away from God and seek solace elsewhere.
- Even Jesus' own disciples abandoned Him in this moment.

"At that point, all the disciples abandoned Jesus and ran away." – Matthew 26:56

- Have you ever **deserted God out of confusion, fear, or grief**?

The Joy of "Sunday"

- If you hold onto the promises of God, you will inevitably make it to **Sunday—the day of rejoicing and freedom.**
- Where in your life do you **personally desire to experience a "Sunday" moment?**

Accountability Check-In

(If pairing with the SoulStrength Fit Workout Program)

- Did you **complete your workouts** this week? What helped you stay on track, or what challenges made it difficult?
- How did you feel about your **nutrition and eating habits** this week? Share a specific example of a day when you felt aligned with your goals or a time when it was challenging to stay on track.

Encourage group members to support one another, share any victories or struggles, and offer **practical encouragement and accountability**.

Closing Prayer & Prayer Requests

Invite each member to share a personal prayer request. Close in prayer, asking God to make His presence abundantly clear in the week ahead and to deepen each person's understanding of His love, grace, and sacrifice.

About the Author

Kelly Wenner is the founder and creator of SoulStrength Fit and SoulStrength Fit Kids. With over two decades of experience in education, fitness, and spiritual development, Kelly has dedicated her life to helping others deepen their faith, honor God in all areas of life, and step into the full potential He has designed for them.

As a faith-based fitness expert and devotional author, Kelly's mission is to inspire and equip individuals to live vibrant, purpose-filled lives rooted in Christ. Through SoulStrength Fit, she combines her passion for physical and spiritual well-being to create programs and devotionals that encourage growth, resilience, and faithfulness.

Come to the Cross reflects Kelly's heart for drawing others into a deeper understanding of Christ's love and sacrifice. She prays this book will encourage readers to reflect on Jesus' final words, embrace the hope of the resurrection, and experience the transforming power of His grace in their daily lives.

Kelly lives in Southern California with her husband and three daughters, where she continues to find joy in serving others and sharing the transformative power of faith.

.

www.ingramcontent.com/pod-product-compliance
Lightning Source LLC
LaVergne TN
LVHW051428080426
835508LV00022B/3288